A Book of Poems

Arthur Leggett

A catalogue record for this book is available from the National Library of Australia

First published 2002 Paperback
Copyright © 2021 Arthur Leggett
All rights reserved.
ISBN: 978-1-922343-94-9

Linellen Press
265 Boomerang Road
Oldbury, Western Australia
www.linellenpress.com.au

CONTENTS

Foreword 5
Sports Car 6
OFFICE MEMOS 8
Earthbound 14
Just Wondering 16
A Letter to Virgillia's Friendly Corner 19
The Illicit Radio 22
Sundown 23
Plain Sailing 24
To Eileen 25
Adoration 26
Friendship 28
To New Grandparents 30
The Kimberleys 31
Aftermath 32
Mustering 34
Drought 36
Geraldton 38
Sunday Afternoon Stroll 40
Summer Idyll 44
6th August 46
Ask Not For Whom 48
About the Author 49

Foreword

They tell me, now, "'tis Autumn-time!"
As if I didn't know
The Heat of Summer's long since gone;
And Spring? Where did it go?
I recollect The Joys of Spring,
Life's Growth stirring - new,
The Blossoming of Youthful Dreams
When all things said were true.
Summer's Heat once held its sway,
Then all was "Effort" and "Persist!"
As I reached out beyond The Edge
Seeking Substance in The Mist.
But now 'tis Autumn! Summer's Torch
I strive to hold up high,
Knowing Time's Hands rest upon my years.
I glide — but cannot fly!

* * *

Sports Car

I have this little motor-car
Which, I'm told, resembles me.
Of sporty lines and full of dash
As anyone can see.

It roars out of the driveway
And tears off down the street,
Shouting at the neighbours,
Calling out, "Beep! Beep!"
It glides up to the corners,
Changes down and moves away,
Its motor joyfully singing,
I'm a true, blue sports coupe.

I took a close look at my car.
I felt I really must.
I noticed, in those 'sporty lines'
There's quite a bit of rust.

The shock absorbers don't absorb
The shocks the way they used to do,
It labours going up a hill
And, sometimes, brakes askew.

It needs a valve grind or new head,
A replacement petrol gauge,
And the clutch is slowly slipping,
But I guess that's just old age.

So, when friends say my sporty car
Closely resembles me,
I thoughtfully just nod my head
And ruefully agree.

* * *

OFFICE MEMOS

To: The Management.
From: The Office Cleaner.

Sir, I wish to comment
On a problem in 'The Loo'.
Two light globes have 'turned it in'
The way they sometimes do.

Now, it may not cause much trouble
While the sun is in full flight,
But contemplate the terror
Which surrounds me in the night.

There's the ever-present danger
Of a stumble in the gloom
As I'm mopping o'er the flooring
Of that tiny, little room.

'Twould be just my luck to trip up
Head first down the drain,
Bump that button as I go
And ne'er be seen again!

* * *

To: The Wind Gods
From: The Office Cleaner.

Oh Thou, Who doth the winds control
Throughout this mighty land,
Let not the east wind blow this night
A-stirring up the sand.
To filter through the office
And spoil my lovely work;
For, if Thou dost, Thou knowest
Thou hast dropped me in the irk!

* * *

To: The Sales Manager
From: The Purchasing Clerk.

Sir, I'm off on two weeks holiday
To Mandurah, down the coast,
Where folks just lay in the sun all day
And the local people boast,

"The fish jump from the water
To take your flamin' bait!
The crabs are there in thousands
And the pubs stay open late!

So, that's where I am going
From the Cup of Life to fill.
I'll think of you while I'm away,
I will — pig's arse I will!

* * *

To: Deidre.
From: The Purchasing Clerk.

Have I, somehow, upset you
In that thoughtless blundering way
For which I'm noted round the office?
'Cos, if I have, just say.

I scarce have seen you smile of late,
There's no Life in your voice.
If I have, somehow, upset you,
It was not done by choice.

No, this is no love poem.
Emotions not its essence.
I needs must come here every day
And I'm conscious of your presence.

* * *

To: Kaye
From: The Purchasing Clerk

Subject: My Retirement.

How do I say, "Farewell" to you
With whom I've worked these years?
Just turn around and walk away?
Pretend it is not tears
Misting eyes which now must grow
More dim each passing year?
Ah; were I blind to-morrow
My sight of you is clear.
For I have seen you beauteous grow
From teenage years to womanhood,
Known your presence daily near
And felt that it was good
To learn your moods,
Share your smiles,
Sense affection – never said –
My dear, how I shall miss you
In the years which lie ahead.

* * *

Earthbound

Sometimes, when digging in the garden
I can hear a jet-plane crawling
Towards the runway of the airport
On the other side of the river.

In my imagination I can see
The humanity-packed, aluminium cylinder crouching;
Flexing its muscles, before commencing
Its roaring, cavalry-like charge
Towards the unseen end of the airstrip
Hidden in the shimmering distance.

"Bring me my Chariots of Fire!"
Roar the engines.
"Faster! Faster!" swish the wheels
"Lift me!" beseech the wings.
The cylinder tilts and the plane,
Snarling free from gravity's influence
Reaches for the sky!

I can see it, now, climbing and circling
Gracefully as it bellows into space,
Continuing its arc to pass directly overhead,
Pointing out to some distant, mysterious
'Where'?

Bali? Singapore? Hong Kong?

I plunge with the spade
To turn the soil
And reveal a worm.
"You and I, my friend,
Have something in common."

* * *

(From The Prisoner of War Camps.)

Just Wondering

Will I ever run home from afar,
Yell through the doorway, "How Ya, Ma?"
See my mother's care-worn face,
Know the touch of her embrace
As she takes my pack and stands awhile
Hiding her tears behind a smile?
Looks in my eyes and smooths my hair
Searching my face for signs of wear
While my heart, in joyful tone,
Sings, "At last I'm home! I'm Home!"

Will I ever see the dawn arise
To flood with light my native skies?
See gum leaves stirring in the breeze?
Hear kookas laughing in the trees?
To greet the dawn with raucous song
Where the river moves along?
Know I'm home and surely, then,
Become a decent citizen
With pride of country, home and race
And be content within my place?

Will I ever know a Life well-spent
To end in peace and sweet content?
Laugh and joke beside a wife
Who has given me some aim in Life?
Know the gentle, sweet caress
Of matehood and its tenderness.
Know the joy she only can
Bestow by whispering, "My man"?

Will I ever know the utmost joy
Of gazing on a tiny boy.
Watch his play, enjoy his fun,
And say with pride, "Yes, that's my son."
See his eyes shine, oh, so glad
As he pulls my hair and calls me, "Dad".
And say to him, "Do you know, son,
You're exceedingly like your lovely mum?"

Will I ever pray with firm conviction,
Without doubt or contradiction,
Knowing He Who gave His Son
Does not consider my Life done?
Who'll lift me from this present strain
To sip The Cup of Life again?
Will I ever kneel in His House of Good
And feel as humble as I should?
Give Him credit for what He's done
And feel my Life has just begun?

Will I ever realise
Things which, now, I visualise?
Will Time, someday, to me reveal
Happiness which now I feel
Lays within the years to come,
When this phase of Life is done.
Will I e'er look back upon this day
And to my inner self shall say,
"The grade was tough; you made it, pal!"
I often wonder if I shall.

* * *

A Letter to Virgillia's Friendly Corner

My Dear Miss Virgillia,
    (I think that is your name)
    I'm living fine and doing well
    And trust that you're the same.
    I'm writing this brief note to you
    Just to let you know
    What happened to your parcel
    Which I got two days ago.

    "Hume Checkers" was the glaring name
    That met our startled gaze,
    And quongdong seeds within a box,
    Which set us all amaze.
    "Quongdong Seeds!" the men all yelled
    And gazed at them with glee.
    "Just the sort of homely things
    Us fellas like to see!"

    They set the boys all talking
    And we spun a bonza tale
    Of Aussies open spaces
    Where the wheat crops never fail.

Where there ain't no droughts or hardships,
Where the land supplies man's needs,
And it's all a flamin' paradise
With mobs of Quongdong Seeds!

Now, Old Bill, who lives away outback,
And here's the pinpoint of my journal,
He looks at them and mutters, hoarse,
"By Cripes! They've got a kernal!"

Before we had quite realised
What that old coot had planned to do
He'd slammed away with the heel of his boot
And put 'Paid' to quite a few.

Old Bill – he's in hospital now,
Queer pains keep shooting through his tummy.
The doctor, who attended him,
Said, "Now this here's funny."

"Me cows sometimes got this complaint
On me farm back in the west.
I think we'll try a dose of salts
And let nature do the rest."

We been four years behind the wire,
A bit down on our luck,
And homely things make homesick blokes
Kind of run amuck.

Old Bill? He'll pull through all right.
Live up to Aussies Name.
I'm sorry, Miss Virgillia,
But thank you just the same.

* * *

The Illicit Radio

Do my ears deceive me
Or rings a melody
From somewhere in the distance
Calling, calling me?

Sings it of home and friendship
Where foreign tongues are not?
It wakes in me fond memories
Of things I'd nigh forgot.

* * *

Sundown

Sometimes, when I feel I am losing my punch
And Life has me getting all rundown,
I make my thoughtful way to the sea
To walk on the beach – just at sundown.

The cry of the gulls, the sound of the surf,
The nudge of the breeze, help me come down
To earth and keep my feet on the ground
When I walk on the beach – just at sundown.

* * *

Plain Sailing

I'm not the wind that fills your sails
Nor the seas o'er which you fly,
Nor the flung spray or the rigging's song
Or the circling seagull's cry.

I'm not blue sky on a summer's day
Or the distance drawing nearer
As the mainland gradually fades astern
While Rottnest's shape grows clearer.

I'm not the sea breeze through your hair,
Or the strumming mains'l – taught set;
Nor the carefree laugh from the shoreline
Sounding clear in the still of the sunset.

So, let me be the moment when
You furl your sails to rest
After some foray on The Sea of Life
That's put you to the test.

Let me firmly grasp your hand
As the ebb is swiftly flowing,
Then plant your feet firm on the ground
And work out where you're going.

* * *

To Eileen

Life
With all its Pleasure-filled, Colourful Moments
Becomes
A Dull, Grey Existence
Without
The Warmth of Your Companionship.
For
You and I
Are
Granted Time to Share with Each Other,
And
I need Your Nearness
Even
As The Dawn needs The Warmth of The Sun
To
Bring forth The Qualities of a New Day

* * *

Adoration

I stood by a lake as the grey light of dawn
Quietly welcomed the oncoming morn;
Awakening birds which took to wing
Searching for a song to sing.

The wild flowers nodded to the morning breeze
Which whispered to the murmuring trees,
Then ran its fingers through my hair.
Somehow I felt that thou wert there.

For thou art as the break of day,
Fragrant, refreshing and cool in your way.
The sky, now brightening all the while,
Is as my heart when thou dost smile.

The soft outline of yon hill's crest
Is contoured shapely as thy breast
And the murmuring sound from the nearby tree
Sounds how I oft wouldst speak to thee.

The lake, hid in mist yet crystal clear,
Is like our affection for each other, dear.
The surface may toss and turn at will
But the depth is always constant still.

I reached out eager, yearning arms,
Longing to embrace your feminine charms,
To hold your softness, caress your hair.
Alas! My arms held empty air.

Although your charm is ever near
And we know of affection for each other, dear,
Thus must it stay and thus will it be,
Yet, my Life is richer for knowing thee.

* * *

Friendship

If I gently took your hand
And never said a word,
Just stood there, quiet, beside you,
Would my thoughts be heard?

Would you feel vibrations there
Which did a message send
To say, "I'm here beside you.
Relax, you're with a friend?"

Let the pressures ease off in your mind.
'Cos I have no intent
To shout demands or bully you
Or to desires give vent.

Let the anxious lines slip from your face
And your voice relax its tension.
Sense emotions coming through
Saying, "Hush! You need not mention

All the hassles which you face
In your life from week to week.
No! Don't say a single word.
There is no need to speak.

Let silence be our mutual voice.
Just sense that I am near.
And, as you find a tiny smile,
I'll wipe away your tear.

* * *

To New Grandparents

Now new Life reaches out its hand
And grasps with tiny fingers
Your hand to seek security;
And oh! The magic lingers.

Not your child but your children's child,
Yet, there is this bond,
Life, from you, has been passed on
Beyond – Beyond – Beyond.

* * *

The Kimberleys

The north so gently touches you
With its infinite blue sky;
The quietness by a river
Where the breeze moves with a sigh.

The feel of awe in gorges.
The colour – the size – the age!
The raucous birds at daybreak
As night slow leaves the stage.

The charm of sleeping out at night,
The brightness of each star,
Just laying there and gazing
And wondering who you are.

This land – those stars – that vastness,
The breeze and quietness, too!
'Tis then you hear The Wogul say,
"You're only passing through."

* * *

Aftermath

(With apologies to 'Banjo' Patterson)

That's when the squatter,
mounted on his thoroughbred,
Said, "What a stupid, damn thing to do!
There's always tucker over at the homestead!
A billy of tea with damper and stew.

Can't help but wonder
what this country's coming to
When a man would rather up and drown
Than be charged for stealing at a billabong
Sheep which sell for a mere half crown!"

The Sergeant,
standing underneath the coolabah,
Said, to himself, "I hate this job.
Tracking down swagmen camped by a billabong,
Knocking off sheep not worth two bob.

I've got to get his body from the waterhole,
Slushing in mud, pulling on a rope!
Dragging for a swagman no one's ever heard about.
Find next of kin. Oh Cripes! Some hope!"

The young trooper said,
when speaking to his older mate
As they headed back to the town,
"Heard him sing a kind of a waltz song,
But never dreamed he was going to drown.

Don't believe in ghosts
which murmur through the rivergums
Or sing around the old billabong,
But I know when I hear the breeze
come a-whispering
I'll always here his waltzing song."

The trooper turned,
looked hard at the waterhole,
Then replied, "Don't ask me how,
But I'll lay a quid his song will be rolling on
Throughout the country a century from now.

Waltzing Matilda! Waltzing Matilda!
You'll come a-waltzing Matilda with me!
And his ghost may be heard
as you wander by that billabong,
You'll come a-waltzing Matilda with me.

* * *

Mustering

Sing me no song of the great outback
Where the skies are not cloudy all day;
Where the stockmen hum a haunting tune
As they amble on their way.

No perfume's on a morning breeze
That's cold as cold can be;
It coats your grub with reddish dust
And floats it on your tea.

The track's not lined by gumtrees
With creeks a-flowing past.
It's miles and miles of mulga scrub
In country harsh and vast.

The sun's climbed high by mid-day,
It's heat the earth does straddle.
The flies are in your eyes and mouth,
And your bum's sore in the saddle.

Dust-covered cattle up ahead
All bellow and they stink.
You reckon you smell much the same;
It makes you stop and think

'N ask, "What am I doing here?
There must be some other way
To make a flamin' living!"
I'll take a look - someday.

But, when the day is over,
The tough times you forget
While the billy water's murmuring
As you roll a cigarette,

'N your dog curls up beside you.
It kind of makes you glad
You're out here in the mulga
Where the life is not too bad.

* * *

Drought

I've just read a bush poem of Lawson's
'tis out through the window I gaze,
Past the back fence and houses nearby
And beyond — to my childhood days.

We sat on the dry River Mehi's banks
And felt the hot wind's searing heat;
We heard the crispy, crackling sound
Of dead gum leaves beneath our bare feet.

The hot wind rustled through river gums
With whispers, seeming to say,
"Be brave. Hang on for another year.
It's going to rain – someday."

And me and me mates sat there in the dust
And wondered just how it would be
If water flowed past our unclad feet
Then made its way out to sea.

In truth, we'd never seen the sea
But Joe would boastfully say,
"It's right around Australia
And the rivers run that way."

"Aw; bet you made that up," we said.
But sure of himself was Joe.
"Nah; I didn't make it up!
I know! That's all! I know!"

"Well, if that's the way the rivers go
When they're flowing fast,
The Mehi doesn't join them.
There's nothing going past.

"Of course there ain't no water!"
Says Joe with deep disdain,
"Before the rivers start to run
You've got to have some rain!"

We looked at the dried-up river's bed,
Felt the hot wind's nudge again,
And wondered what it looked like,
This funny stuff called 'Rain'.

* * *

Geraldton

I climbed the big hill by Geraldton town
Where, from its bluff height, I quietly looked down,
saw the sun sink slow, all red, to the sea
And felt my Creator was quite close to me.

Each chimney a grey-coloured banner unfurled,
The sea a mist blanket likewise uncurled.
'Twas one of those days you just can't forget
Nor witness its passing without some regret.

A day which began e'er morning's first light
Had properly dispersed the shades of the night
When crayboats hauled their anchors aweigh
As their motors barked "Welcome" to oncoming day.

The sun came up o'er the hills to the east
And smiled when he saw what a beautiful feast
Of colour this township of Geraldton gave;
He sent his light westward and kissed every wave.

Yea! Every wave danced and glistened with glee
To transfuse their beauty all over the sea
Which thundered a welcome to fast-rising day
Out on the reefs in a flurry of spray!

The eastern hills, all matted green,
Now presented a promising scene
Of crops which will grow and sheep which will graze
Long after we have ended our days.

Good people, engaged in worldly commerce,
I beg of you 'Pause'; and you might do worse
Than to stand like some boat
                      with its sails softly luffing
And see what God gives you, in this town,
                            for nothing!

* * *

Sunday Afternoon Stroll

"Let's go for a walk," my wife said,
"For an hour. Let's leave the house
And walk along the cycle path
By the old East Perth Powerhouse."

The powerhouse stands by the river"s edge
But there's no machinery hum.
It's not been used for many years,
Its usefulness is done.

And, as I gazed at its massive bulk
With its impressive chimney stack,
My mind commencing meandering
Away back down Life's Track.

To the days when I was seventeen,
Standing in the foreman's shed.
"So you heat rivets?" he booms out.
"Yes, Mr. Scott," I said.

"Wot was the last job you was on?
I've got to know your worth.
Suppose you tell me where you was?
This is the only site in Perth."

"I've been on the fields at Laverton
Working with a rivet crew.
The job cut out. I'm back in Perth.
They said I should see you."

We stood there, silent, for a while;
Him pondering out the door,
Me waiting anxiously
And gazing at the floor.

I didn't know that he knew
I'd been up there milking cows,
Living in a hessian shed
With a roof of bush and boughs.

I didn't know that he knew
My Dad was slowly dying.
My Mum kept boarders in our house,
And that's why I was lying.

"Tell you what I'll do," he said,
"I'll put you on as 'hired',
We'll see just how you shape up.
If you're no good – you're fired!"

He introduced me to the riveter,
Who guessed I didn't have a clue.
"Let's get up on the job," he said,
"I'll show you what to do."

That's how I first met up with Jeff
Who came from The U.S.A.
And Gus Levitzke from Midland
Who quietly said, "G'day."

Jeff handled the pneumatic gun,
Gus backed up rivets, hot and round,
I cranked my forge upon three planks
Two hundred feet above the ground!

The three of us made quite a crew
And there's something we can show!
We built that bloody chimney
Over fifty years ago!

It's sad to think that old Jeff died
Of cancer in the kidney,
And Gus, with his youthful vigour,
Went down aboard 'The Sydney'.

And I am just an old bloke
Wondering where the years have gone
As I walk, in the cool of the evening,
On the banks of The River Swan.

* * *

Summer Idyll

I was cleaning out my swimming pool
On a sunny afternoon.
The warm sun soft caressed my back
And the garden was in bloom.

When I heard a little 'Plop!'
In the water, near the brink.
The first grasshopper of the summer
Had crash-landed in the drink.

At first he floated upright
Then rolled on to his side'
His jumper-legs a-kicking,
His distress he could not hide.

He struggled there quite desperately
But all to no avail;
His outstretched wings forlornly wet,
As he slowly wagged his tail.

His big, black eyes looked into mine,
I'm sure I saw him frown,
And I heard his voice a-gurgling,
"Hey! You going to let me drown?"

So, I scooped him up out of the pool
And, as he looked me in the eye,
I squashed him underneath my foot
And said, "Die, you bastard, die!"

* * *

6th August

Some of you young folk sicken me
When you survey the past from here – today.
Ignoring history as it was,
The part us old blokes had to play.

Have you not heard of nurses
Herded out into the water
Then machine-gunned for no reason
But indifferent, callous slaughter?

Have you all forgotten scenes
From The Railroads murderous toil?
The starving mob in Changi Gaol?
The dead on Ambon's soil?

Let me tell you who they were,
These ulcer-ridden shapes.
Kicked and tortured – bashed to death.
They were my teenage mates!

The chaps whom I played cricket with
Or swelled the football's cheers.
We sailed our yacht upon The Swan,
Laughed together. Drank our beers.

Have you forgotten Darwin Town was bombed?
Broome and Wyndham wrecked?
New Guinea nearly over-run?
Forgotten who was next?

The Invader pounded at the door!
Reached out with yellow hand
To raze my city, rape my kin
And take my native land!

Now you cry for the vanquished!
Shout "Shame" with great aplomb.
Condemn my generation
And its immoral atom bomb.

A war's a bloody awful thing
In which Man murders Man.
Yet, fifty years along Life's Track,
No one gives a damn!

But, before you weep for the enemy
And mourn his tragic cost,
Sit down and quietly ask yourself,
"My God! What if we'd lost?"

* * *

Ask Not For Whom

To whom can I sing my love songs
Now that my youth is past?
Why do I sing so desperately
Those songs which did not last?

Who stays to hear my love songs
Since ruthless Time has found me
Stepping carefully 'midst the years
Now grown like weeds around me?

Where is The Wind that once did blow
Boisterous with Desire?
The Hot Pursuit? The Soaring Heat?
The Quenching of The Fire?

Where is The Brook that once did flow
Past my feet as I, content,
Pushed my paper boat midstream
And cared not where it went?

Ah, 'tis gone beyond recall.
Upon Life's Stream 'tis journeying.
Bobbing downstream to the Misty Years,
And The Brook keeps murmuring –
                                      murmuring.

* * *

About the Author

Arthur Leggett is a 'Baby Boomer' from the 1914-1918 War which means he has been around for some time. At the time of this re-publication, 102 years.

He is a member of The Bush Poets and Yarn Spinners Association and frequently recites at The Peninsular Folk Club.

Numerous poems and articles have been published during recent years in club newsletters and various anthologies.

Apart from *A Book of Poems*, Arthur has also written his autobiography *Don't Cry for Me*.

* * *

www.ingramcontent.com/pod-product-compliance
Lightning Source LLC
Chambersburg PA
CBHW021159080526
44588CB00008B/423